Patrick Henry

*The inspiring true-life story of the
leader whose oratory set
young America aflame*

DRAMATIZED IN
ALL-PICTORIAL PRESENTATION

FOR IMPROVED
AWARENESS BOOK
READING

Davco Publishers
SKOKIE, ILLINOIS 60076

CONSULTANTS

SARA THROOP, PH.D.
> *Youngstown State University*
> *Youngstown, Ohio*

JOAN DUFF KISE, PH.D.
> *Elementary Education Department*
> *Kent State University*
> *Kent, Ohio*

IDA S. MELTZER, B.A.
> *Supervisor Language Arts*
> *Marine Park Junior High School*
> *Brooklyn, New York*

SYLVIA E. DAVIS, M.S.A.E.
> *Chairman Art Department*
> *Waller High School*
> *Chicago, Illinois*

MORRIS R. BUSKE, M.A.
> *Instructor Social Studies*
> *Department*
> *Triton College*
> *River Grove, Illinois*

DOROTHY L. GROSS, B.S.M.S.
> *Instructor Art Department*
> *Detroit Public Schools*
> *Detroit, Michigan*

EDITORIAL AND ART

Executive Editor

> JANET TEGLAND, M.A.
> *Coordinator Learning*
> *Disabilities Department*
> *Top of the World School*
> *Laguna Beach Unified School*
> *District*
> *Laguna Beach, California*
> *Instructor Creative Writing*
> *Saddleback Community College*
> *Mission Viejo, California*

Artists

> MELVIN KEEFER
> CARLOS NORTE
> BARBARA FERENCZ
> PAT LOZARO

Historical Researchers

> THOMAS MCLAUGHLIN
> BARBARA MCCORMICK
> BERTHA RABENS

Art and Editorial Production

> HOWARD PARKS
> CARYL KURTZMAN
> ARLINE BLOCK
> GAIL GOLDBERG
> JOSEPH POSTILION
> RONALD FALK

© MCMLXXVII Davco Publishers
Skokie, Illinois 60076

Library of Congress catalog card No. 77-087926

ISBN No. 0-89233-013-9

I know not what course others may take, but as for me, give me liberty or give me death!

PATRICK HENRY
At Virginia Convention,
March 23, 1775

Table of Contents

On September 5, 1774, statesmen from the thirteen American colonies met in Philadelphia to decide what action to take against England's unfair treatment of the colonies.

Among the statesmen was Patrick Henry of Virginia—already well known for his inspiring speeches against the British.

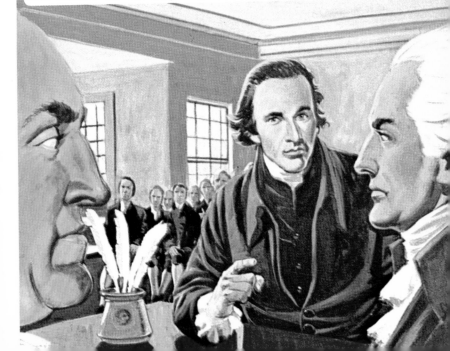

Many men at the First Continental Congress wanted America to remain a part of England.

We cannot break our ties with our mother country.

We must have a voice in how we are governed. But we cannot exist apart from England.

Patrick Henry believed the colonies had no choice but to separate from England.

England will never be fair to the colonies. We must be independent.

Boston patriot Sam Adams introduced a plan drawn up by the people of Suffolk County, Massachusetts.

We must refuse to pay taxes to England.

And we must stop all trade with England at once.

The Suffolk County Resolutions were passed by the Congress.

Henry helped write a letter to the king of England, telling him what actions the colonies were taking.

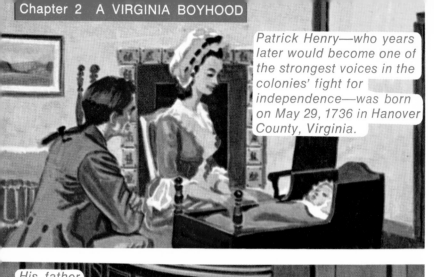

Patrick Henry—who years later would become one of the strongest voices in the colonies' fight for independence—was born on May 29, 1736 in Hanover County, Virginia.

His father served as chief justice of the Hanover County Court.

Sssh, Pat. Come back. Your father is busy.

There were no public schools in Virginia in the 1700s—so Patrick was sent to a private school until he was ten years old.

Master Henry! Your father expects you to learn to read and write. And I intend to see that you *do*.

When he was eleven, he returned home . . .

. . . where he was taught Latin and Greek by his father.

The Roman senators were great speech-makers, Pat. Think about that when you are practicing your Latin.

What do those words mean, Pat?

It's from Horace. 'And for our country, 'tis a bliss to die.'

When Pat was fourteen, his mother took him to hear a visiting preacher deliver a sermon.

His name is Reverend Samuel Davies, Pat. His sermons are supposed to be very exciting.

Patrick was deeply moved by the sermon of Reverend Davies.

And I say to you that good *will* triumph.

He was the best speaker I ever heard. It wasn't just what he said, but how he said it . . . the way he moved his hands.

When he was not studying, Patrick helped his father manage the land owned by the Henrys . . .

. . . and spent many hours enjoying his two favorite pastimes: hunting . . .

. . . and playing the violin.

1

When Patrick was fifteen, he became an apprentice in a crossroads store near his home.

You'll work for Mr. Thompson for a year. I want you to learn how to run a business.

Patrick worked hard for Mr. Thompson . . .

. . . but more than anything else, he enjoyed listening to the talk of the people who gathered in the store.

It seems to me we could make some of our own tools here in America, instead of buying them all from England.

When Patrick's year in Mr. Thompson's store had ended, his father talked to him.

I'll try hard to succeed.

I'll give you land and lumber to build your own store. I want you to take your brother in as partner.

Patrick was determined to make good as a storekeeper.

I hope I can make enough to support a family. I want to marry Sarah Shelton.

He started building his store.

THE HENRY BROS. MERCHANTS

Patrick enjoyed being a storekeeper. He kept his store open late at night so that he could listen to the farmers who came from miles around to sit and talk.

Come in, come in. I have a new copy of the *Virginia Gazette.*

Not enough rain this year. Tobacco crop is going to be bad.

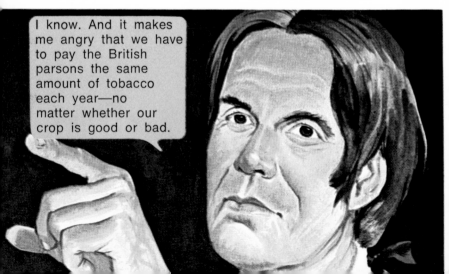

I know. And it makes me angry that we have to pay the British parsons the same amount of tobacco each year—no matter whether our crop is good or bad.

Patrick didn't like to ask the farmers to pay their bills when the tobacco crop was poor.

So many people have no money. But they need supplies from the store. I can't turn them away.

Patrick was forced to close his store a year after he opened it.

CLOSED UNTIL FURTHER NOTICE

But he continued to see Sarah Shelton.

I have no money, no land, and no job, Sarah. But I can't give up the hope of asking you to be my wife.

Let's talk to my father, Pat. I know he'll help us.

I always meant to give the Pine Slash farm to Sarah. So I'll make it your wedding present. I'm sure you'll do well as a farmer, Pat.

Patrick and Sarah were married in 1754 . . .

. . . and Patrick worked hard as a farmer.

But in 1757, Pine Slash burned down.

I'll think of something.

Our home, our furniture, all gone. What will we do now?

Patrick moved his family into a small cabin on the Pine Slash land.

We'll be living here only a little while, Sarah, I promise.

He sold some of the Pine Slash land and opened another store.

At the same time, he worked the remaining land of the farm at Pine Slash.

But again, the tobacco crop was poor— and Patrick was forced to close his store.

Everything I've tried to do has failed.

In 1760, Patrick decided to study law.

What would you think of me becoming a lawyer, Sarah?

I think it's a wonderful idea. You already know Latin and Greek. And you're a wonderful speaker.

For the next eight months, Patrick was a farmer during the day—and a law student at night.

In March, 1760, he rode to Williamsburg to take his law examinations.

The men who examined him were four of Virginia's finest lawyers.

One of the examiners refused to pass him.

I'm sorry, Mr. Henry. You must study the law much longer before I can pass you.

Another examiner agreed to pass him—on one condition.

I must have your promise that you will continue to study your law.

Two other examiners passed him.

I believe you will do honor to your profession.

He hurried to tell Sarah.

I passed! I passed!

Henry began to practice law at once. Farmers and plantation owners brought him their legal work.

Henry's a lawyer now?

Seems to me he'd win any jury with his grand way of speaking.

He drafted wills...

I want all my land to go to my oldest son.

...and defended debtors.

He said he'd take my breed sow in payment, and he took her. But she died, and now he wants more.

He spent many days traveling on horseback from county to county to try his cases.

In 1763, against the advice of his friends, Patrick agreed to defend the people of Louisa County against the Reverend James Maury. He was demanding extra payments for a year in which the tobacco crop had been poor.

You can't possibly win, Pat.

I can try.

His own father, John Henry, was going to be the judge in the trial.

Pat, you know I have already ruled that the people must pay Reverend Maury.

Yes, father. But your ruling didn't say how much.

Reverend Maury was certain he would win.

The king of England has already ruled in my favor. And so has Henry's own father. I can't lose.

In 1758, colonial statesmen in the Virginia Assembly passed the Two Penny Act—setting the price of tobacco at two pence a pound in years when the tobacco crop was poor.

It isn't fair.

Everywhere else, the price of tobacco is higher.

Because church leaders were paid with tobacco instead of money, they felt they were being cheated when the price of tobacco was held down.

One clergyman was so angry, he sailed to England to plead his case before the king.

On July 4, 1759, the king of England declared the Two Penny Act illegal.

Virginia had no right to pass such a law.

Reverend Maury was trying to collect the money he felt he should have been paid in 1758.

The money is rightfully mine.

Henry did not believe the king of England had the right to change a law passed by Virginians for Virginians.

We can make better laws for ourselves than a king can on the other side of the ocean.

Many Virginians agreed with Henry— but were surprised that he would dare to speak so boldly against England.

This is one trial I'm not going to miss.

When Patrick Henry entered court on the day of the trial, twenty church leaders sat on a bench in the front of the courtroom.

Reverend Maury's lawyer spoke first.

The people owe Reverend Maury 264 pounds.

Then it was Henry's turn.

A king is sworn to protect his people. The Two Penny Act was a good law. A king who wanted to protect his people would not have removed it.

Treason! He is speaking treason.

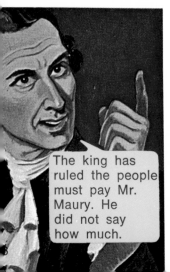

The king has ruled the people must pay Mr. Maury. He did not say how much.

The jury returned in five minutes.

We order the collector to pay Reverend Maury exactly one cent.

Two years later, Henry was elected a member of the Virginia House of Burgesses.

At last I shall have a voice in making laws for Virginia Colony.

He took his seat in the House of Burgesses on May 20, 1765.

Who's that?

Patrick Henry. They say he has quite a way with words.

Nine days later, the Virginians received word that England had passed the Stamp Act.

A stamp is being placed on all paper goods— newspapers, legal papers, even calendars. And the British expect us to pay for the stamps with gold or silver.

Patrick was angry.

But we have no choice *but* to accept the tax.

If we accept this tax, we are giving up our rights as free men to be taxed only with our own consent.

27

Henry stayed up all night writing down his ideas against the Stamp Act.

He presented five resolutions against the act in the House of Burgesses the next day.

Only Virginians have the right to tax Virginia.

The burgesses all stood. Half of them cheered Henry, and half of them were shouting in anger.

Hurrah for Henry!

Treason!

If *this* be treason, make the most of it!

On May 30, the House voted on—and passed—Henry's resolutions.

It was a close vote, Pat. But you won.

News of Henry's resolutions spread to all the colonies.

At last someone has dared to speak out against the British.

All of the colonies except Georgia refused to obey the Stamp Act.

NO STAMPS

No stamps! No stamps! No stamps!

A year later, England repealed the law.

King George has taken back the Stamp Act.

Henry was regarded as a hero by his fellow Virginians.

But before many years had passed, there was serious trouble with England again.

VIRGINIA GAZET

ENGLAND LEVIES
NEW TAXES WIT
TOWNSHEND ACT

Colonists in Rhode Island burned a British ship.

Virginia statesmen— including Henry and Jefferson— held a secret meeting in March, 1773.

The colonies must inform each other about unfair acts by the British.

Committees of Correspondence were formed between the colonies.

I'll tell the people in Massachusetts that Rhode Island will join them.

When the British gave a monopoly on tea to the East India Company, patriots in Boston dumped shiploads of British tea into the harbor.

The British declared the port of Boston closed until the tea was paid for.

Virginia's colonial leaders held a special meeting —and agreed to support the people of Boston.

We will not buy any more British goods.

They also elected Virginia's delegates to the First Continental Congress September 5, 1774, which was called to discuss colonial grievances against England.

I must go to Philadelphia, Sarah. Leaders from all the colonies are meeting.

3

Henry rode to Philadelphia with another Virginia delegate, George Washington.

In Philadelphia, he spoke out loudly against the British.

We must not ask for peace. We must demand our rights!

When he returned home, he found Sarah gravely ill.

I'm afraid there is no hope.

Sarah died, and Henry mourned her deeply.

Shortly after Sarah's death, Henry inspired his countrymen to arm themselves for war with the British.

He speaks as man was never known to speak before.

Angry at the colonists, the British governor of Virginia seized all the gunpowder in the state.

I want that gunpowder moved to Norfolk.

Henry gathered volunteer soldiers from all over Hanover County.

We will march on Williamsburg and take back our gunpowder.

While he was preparing his soldiers to fight, a messenger arrived.

The gunpowder is gone. But the British governor is sending money to pay for it.

Henry accepted the money— but the angry governor wrote a letter to the king of England.

Henry is a dangerous man who excites the people to revolt.

When he was elected a delegate to the Second Continental Congress in May, 1775, Henry knew that the British governor was angry enough to arrest him.

We thought you might like some company on your ride to Philadelphia, Pat.

By the time he reached the Potomac River ferry at the Virginia border, he was surrounded by young colonists who wanted to protect him.

At the Second Continental Congress, he worked for the election of George Washington as president of the Congress.

Washington could unite us all.

When he returned to Virginia, Henry was named commander in chief of Virginia's army.

They're eager to fight. I hope the British attack. We'll show them how we fight.

When Virginia's army joined the Continental army, Henry resigned.

I feel I can serve my country better as a lawmaker than as a general.

He was named a delegate to the Virginia Convention in May, 1776—where he played a major role in writing Virginia's first constitution and bill of rights . . .

. . . and where his plan for Virginia's declaration of independence from England was presented

. . . and accepted.

Henry was elected the first governor of the state of Virginia in June, 1776.

He worked hard to make sure that Virginia played a major role in fighting the Revolutionary War.

We need to enlist 6,000 men for Washington's army —and 5,000 men for our own state militia.

He traveled all over the state encouraging the men of Virginia to join the army.

Washington is a Virginian and he needs you.

His speeches inspired hundreds of men to enlist.

I was going to stay home and tend my crops until I heard Pat Henry. He sure has a way with words.

ENLIST NOW

He saw to it that soldiers from Virginia had shoes and clothes when they joined the army.

When Washington's army was starving during the cruel winter at Valley Forge . . .

. . . Henry made certain they received beef cattle from the state of Virginia.

What do you mean the British will pay more? I don't want to hear it! Your countrymen are starving at Valley Forge!

He encouraged mine owners of his state to mine more lead for ammunition.

We can't defeat the British without bullets.

He imported gunpowder from any country that would sell it to Virginia.

Spain must have gunpowder for sale. Buy it!

In 1777, he met the daughter of a Virginia colonel.

I have heard you have no time for dancing, Governor Henry.

At the moment, my time is yours.

They were married on October 9, 1778.

Despite the great expenses caused by the war, Henry did not wish to impose heavy taxes on his people.

James Madison and Thomas Jefferson say you will *have* to ask the people to pay more taxes.

I know what it is to be poor. I will *not* tax my people any more than they can bear.

Jefferson and Madison were angry.

How does he expect Virginia to pay her debts?

But the poor people of Virginia admired him.

He's a backcountry man, just like us.

Governor Henry supported George Rogers Clark's plan to win the Northwest Territory.

If we drive the British out of the land between the Ohio and the Mississippi rivers, our frontier will be safe.

Clark was successful, and Virginia claimed the land between the Ohio and the Mississippi.

CANADA

MISSISSIPPI RIVER

MISSOURI RIVER

OHIO RIVER

ATLANTIC OCEAN

Maryland also wanted the land. It refused to sign the Articles of Confederation that would unite the states.

Then let's give the land to the Confederation Congress. In time of war, we must unite.

Under Virginia law, governors could not serve more than three consecutive terms. Thomas Jefferson was elected governor in 1779.

But Henry continued to serve Virginia in the state legislature.

Welcome back, Pat.

In 1780, he introduced a bill to give the governor of Virginia more power.

The governor must have the power to raise an army—and the power to punish people who hurt the war effort.

After the Revolutionary War, James Madison introduced a bill to raise taxes in Virginia. Henry opposed it.

The backcountry people are not rich like the plantation owners. To tax them more would be wrong.

The people of Virginia reelected Henry governor in 1785.

I didn't think I'd be living in the governor's mansion again.

The people still want you, Patrick.

Henry took office at the same time that John Jay was in Spain trying to draw up a treaty between Spain and America.

When Henry learned that Jay's treaty would deny American rights on the Mississippi River, he was furious.

Jay is a fool.

He spoke out loudly against Jay's treaty.

We cannot approve such a treaty. Spain would take over our western frontier.

He also found himself opposing the ideas of his fellow Virginians Jefferson and Madison.

They are trying to draw up a plan so that all the states will be ruled by a strong, federal government. I don't like it.

America needs new laws. Virginia needs new laws. But there is no point in trying to change Virginia's laws while Henry is still alive.

I wish we had his support. The people *listen* to him.

We fought a war so that the states would have the right to govern themselves.

A constitutional convention, where the states would meet to consider a new form of government, was called in 1787. Henry was elected a delegate, but refused to attend.

I cannot take part in any meeting that will take power away from the states.

James Madison and George Washington attended the convention as delegates from Virginia.

Washington was named chairman of the convention.

Gentlemen, you do me great honor.

James Madison had a plan for a whole new form of government.

I propose a Congress made up of two houses.

On September 24, Washington sent Henry a copy of the new Constitution —based on Madison's plan.

Henry read the new Constitution carefully...

...and wrote Washington that he would not be able to support it.

"...it is with great regret..."

Under the new Constitution, the states would have no power.

In December, 1787, Madison wrote Jefferson.

"...Patrick Henry, more than any other, is the man most likely to bring about the defeat of the Constitution."

Virginia's leading statesmen were divided into three groups with differing feelings about the Constitution.

One group—including James Madison and John Marshall—hoped the Constitution would be quickly approved by all the states.

Another group—including Virginia's governor, Edmund Randolph—wanted to be able to amend the Constitution before it was approved.

The third group—with Henry as its spokesman—was against the Constitution.

S FOR LIBERTY

HENRY OPPOSES CONSTITUTION

When each state decided to have a ratifying convention to vote on whether or not they wanted to approve the Constitution—Henry ran as a delegate from his county.

I wish to announce that I am running.

Henry won the election—and James Madison was worried.

I know the people from the north will support the Constitution. But in the south, the people will do whatever Henry tells them to do.

Madison worked hard to persuade the men who had not made up their minds—particularly Governor Randolph—to vote for the Constitution.

If Henry has his way, this nation will become thirteen separate nations.

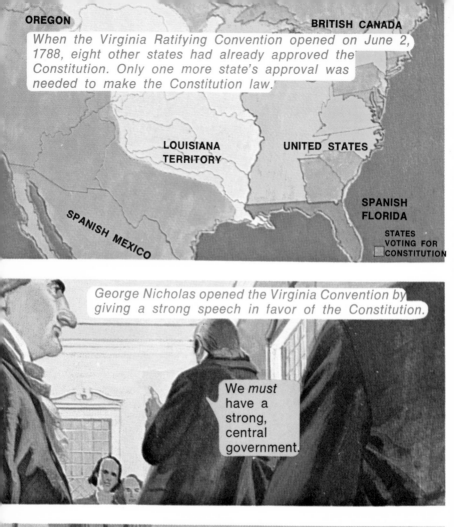

OREGON

BRITISH CANADA

When the Virginia Ratifying Convention opened on June 2, 1788, eight other states had already approved the Constitution. Only one more state's approval was needed to make the Constitution law.

LOUISIANA TERRITORY

UNITED STATES

SPANISH MEXICO

SPANISH FLORIDA

STATES VOTING FOR CONSTITUTION

George Nicholas opened the Virginia Convention by giving a strong speech in favor of the Constitution.

We *must* have a strong, central government.

When Nicholas had finished, Henry rose at once to present his views.

Why does the Constitution open with the words "We the people" instead of "We the *states*"?

A majority of men in the new Congress could pass a law that would be harmful to Virginia.

Do you know that leaders of eight states were in favor of Jay's treaty with Spain that would have stopped Americans from shipping on the Mississippi River?

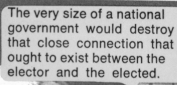

The very size of a national government would destroy that close connection that ought to exist between the elector and the elected.

During the Revolution . . . when the genius of Virginia called on us for liberty . . . On this awful occasion, did you want a federal government?

But in the Virginia General Assembly of 1788, Henry made it clear he was not through fighting.

The Constitution *must* be amended before the new government begins.

And he made certain that two of his supporters were elected to the U.S. Senate.

RICHARD HENRY LEE 98
WILLIAM GRAYTON 86
JAMES MADISON 77
LLY BOARD

Ten amendments to the Constitution were sent to the states for approval September 25, 1789.

I had hoped for even more than these.

Henry resigned from public office in 1791. He returned to his home in Charlotte County, Virginia.

He wrote James Monroe, expressing his feelings about the new government.

"...since we are all embarked, it is natural to care for the crazy machine..."

He returned to his law practice...

...and found himself much in demand as a lawyer.

I want you to join me in defending the right of Virginians not to pay their prewar debts to the British.

Henry shut himself in his office for days to research this important case.

Patrick, you must get some rest.

Not yet, not yet.

When the trial began, Henry gave one of his most inspiring speeches.

You all know the pain and devastation caused in this land by the war with the British.

Had Virginia lost the war, would the British have paid debts they owed Virginians? They would *not*.

Moved by his words, all of the judges ruled in Henry's favor.

Henry is an orator indeed.

President Washington wanted Henry to return to public office.

We need Henry's voice in our government.

I agree.

In 1795, Washington offered Henry an important position.

Washington wants me to become his secretary of state. I cannot.

Washington then offered him a position as justice of the Supreme Court. Henry again refused.

He says his health is too poor to permit it.

Many Federalists wanted him to run for President in 1796.

Much as I would like to defeat Jefferson, I must say no.

But Washington kept urging.

You *must* use your influence against the Democratic-Republicans.

Henry agreed to run for the Virginia legislature in 1799.

Do you think you are well enough, Patrick?

I don't know. I guess I'll soon find out.

He again inspired the people of Virginia with his speeches.

He's as good as he ever was. There'll never be another like Henry.

He won the election easily.

But Henry died on June 6, 1799, before he could take office. He was 63 years old.

The newspapers reflected the feelings of the people for Patrick Henry.

June 14, 1799

Mourn Virginia Mourn!
Your Henry is gone!
As long as our rivers flow,
or mountains stand -- so long
will your excellence an worth
be the theme of homage and
endearment, and Virginia,
bearing in mind her loss, will
say to rising generations,
imitate my HENRY.

Rockland county, Virgi
will go to the legislatu
aining of t

He was mourned by the people of Virginia and throughout the other states.

To the Memory
of
PATRICK HENRY
BORN
MAY 29, 1736
DIED
JUNE 6, 1799
Fame His Best Epitaph

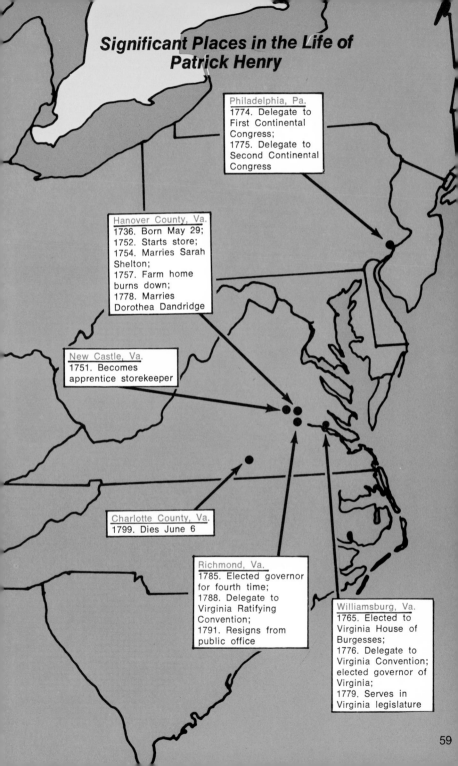

Significant Places in the Life of Patrick Henry

Philadelphia, Pa.
1774. Delegate to First Continental Congress;
1775. Delegate to Second Continental Congress

Hanover County, Va.
1736. Born May 29;
1752. Starts store;
1754. Marries Sarah Shelton;
1757. Farm home burns down;
1778. Marries Dorothea Dandridge

New Castle, Va.
1751. Becomes apprentice storekeeper

Charlotte County, Va.
1799. Dies June 6

Richmond, Va.
1785. Elected governor for fourth time;
1788. Delegate to Virginia Ratifying Convention;
1791. Resigns from public office

Williamsburg, Va.
1765. Elected to Virginia House of Burgesses;
1776. Delegate to Virginia Convention; elected governor of Virginia;
1779. Serves in Virginia legislature

Historical Events During the

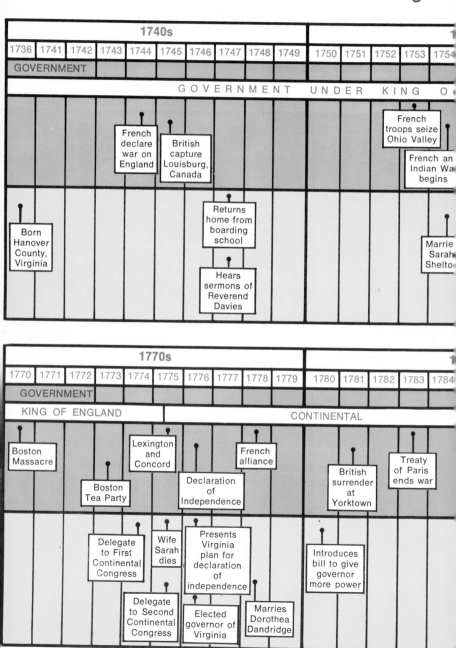

1740s										1				
1736	1741	1742	1743	1744	1745	1746	1747	1748	1749	1750	1751	1752	1753	1754
GOVERNMENT														

GOVERNMENT UNDER KING O

- French declare war on England
- British capture Louisburg, Canada
- French troops seize Ohio Valley
- French an Indian Wa begins
- Born Hanover County, Virginia
- Returns home from boarding school
- Hears sermons of Reverend Davies
- Marrie Sarah Shelto

1770s										1				
1770	1771	1772	1773	1774	1775	1776	1777	1778	1779	1780	1781	1782	1783	1784
GOVERNMENT														

KING OF ENGLAND   CONTINENTAL

- Boston Massacre
- Boston Tea Party
- Lexington and Concord
- Declaration of Independence
- French alliance
- British surrender at Yorktown
- Treaty of Paris ends war
- Delegate to First Continental Congress
- Wife Sarah dies
- Presents Virginia plan for declaration of independence
- Introduces bill to give governor more power
- Delegate to Second Continental Congress
- Elected governor of Virginia
- Marries Dorothea Dandridge

Lifetime of Patrick Henry

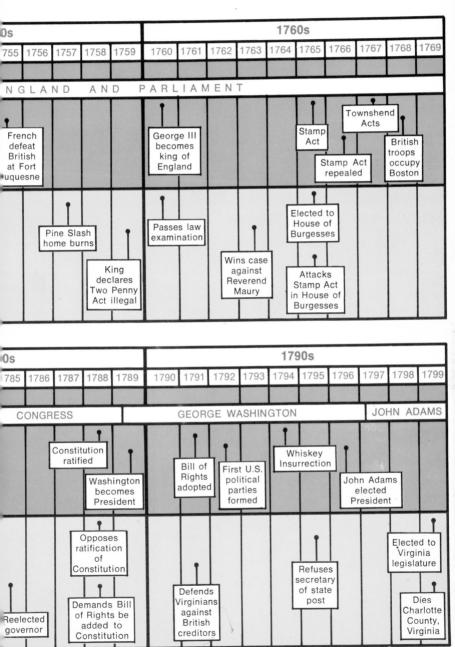

1750s 1755 | 1756 | 1757 | 1758 | 1759

1760s 1760 | 1761 | 1762 | 1763 | 1764 | 1765 | 1766 | 1767 | 1768 | 1769

ENGLAND AND PARLIAMENT

French defeat British at Fort Duquesne

George III becomes king of England

Stamp Act

Townshend Acts

Stamp Act repealed

British troops occupy Boston

Pine Slash home burns

King declares Two Penny Act illegal

Passes law examination

Wins case against Reverend Maury

Elected to House of Burgesses

Attacks Stamp Act in House of Burgesses

1780s 1785 | 1786 | 1787 | 1788 | 1789

1790s 1790 | 1791 | 1792 | 1793 | 1794 | 1795 | 1796 | 1797 | 1798 | 1799

CONGRESS GEORGE WASHINGTON JOHN ADAMS

Constitution ratified

Washington becomes President

Bill of Rights adopted

First U.S. political parties formed

Whiskey Insurrection

John Adams elected President

Opposes ratification of Constitution

Reelected governor

Demands Bill of Rights be added to Constitution

Defends Virginians against British creditors

Refuses secretary of state post

Elected to Virginia legislature

Dies Charlotte County, Virginia

61

GLOSSARY

The meanings and pronunciations of words found in this book

amend *(ə-mĕnd´)*
to alter a legislative measure by adding, deleting, or rephrasing

apprentice *(ə-prĕn´tĭs)*
one bound by a legal agreement to work for another for a specific amount of time in return for instruction in a trade

approved *(ə-prōōvd´)*
confirmed or consented to officially; considered right or good

backcountry *(băk´kŭn-trē)*
rural, thinly settled areas

bliss *(blĭs)*
serene happiness

burgess *(bûr´jĭs)*
a member of the lower house of the colonial legislature of Maryland or Virginia

colonel *(kûr´nəl)*
an officer ranking just above a lieutenant-colonel and just below a brigadier general

commission *(kə-mĭsh´ən)*
a fee or percentage allowed to someone for his services

consecutive *(kən-sĕk´yə-tĭv)*
following successively without interruption

correspondence
(kôr-rə-spŏn´dəns)
communication by the exchange of letters

course *(kôrs)*
route or path

debtor *(dĕt´ər)*
one who owes something to another

delegate *(dĕl´ə-gāt)*
a person authorized to act as representative for another or others

devastation *(dĕv-ə-stā´shən)*
the act of devastating; laying waste or ruining

differing *(dĭf´ər-ĭng)*
being unlike; disagreeing

draft *(drăft)*
to draw up; compose

embarked *(ĕm-bärkd´)*
went aboard a vessel

encouraging *(ĕn-kûr´ə-jĭng)*
permitting one to be confident or hopeful

endearment *(ĕn-dîr´mənt)*
an expression of affection

enlist *(ĕn-lĭst´)*
to enter the armed forces voluntarily

exist *(ĕg-zĭst´)*
to have life; live

ferry *(fĕr´ē)*
a commercial service for transporting people, vehicles, or goods across a body of water

frontier *(frŭn-tîr´)*
a region just beyond or at the edge of a settled area

genius *(jēn´yəs)*
exceptional talent

homage *(hŏm´ĭj)*
honor or respect paid publicly to a person

influence *(ĭn´flōō-əns)*
a power indirectly affecting a person or a course of events

inspiring *(ĭn-spī´rĭng)*
stimulating to an indicated feeling or action; rousing

major *(mā´jər)*
greater in importance

mansion *(măn´shən)*
a large, stately house

militia *(mə-lĭsh´ə)*
a citizen army, as opposed to professional soldiers

GLOSSARY

objected *(ə b-jĕk′tĭd)*
presented an opposing argument;
expressed disapproval

opposing *(ə -pō′zĭng)*
in conflict with; against

orator *(ôr′ə -tə r)*
a person skilled in the art of public
address

parson *(pär′sə n)*
a clergyman with control of a parish

pastime *(păs′tĭm)*
an activity that occupies one's time
pleasantly; something that interests
or amuses

patriot *(pā′trē-ə t)*
a person who loves, supports, and
defends his country

plantation *(plăn-tā′shə n)*
a large estate or farm on which
crops such as cotton, tobacco, and
sugar are grown

profession *(prə-fĕsh′ə n)*
an occupation or vocation requiring
training in the liberal arts or the
sciences and advanced study in a
specialized field

propose *(prə-pōz′)*
to put forward for consideration or
adoption; suggest

ratify *(răt′ə -fĭ)*
to give formal sanction to; approve

repeal *(rĭ-pēl′)*
to withdraw or annul officially;
revoke; rescind

research *(rĭ-sûrch′)*
to investigate in a scholarly or
scientific way

resigned *(rĭ-zīnd′)*
gave up a job or office; quit

resolution *(rĕz-ə -lōō′shə n)*
a formal statement of a decision or
expression of opinion before or
adopted by an assembly

revolt *(rĭ- vōlt′)*
to rebel or mutiny

senator *(sĕn′ə -tə r)*
a member of a senate

sow *(sou)*
an adult female hog

spokesman *(spōks′mə n)*
a person who speaks in behalf of
another or others

statesmen *(stāts′mĭn)*
leaders in national or international
affairs

tend *(tĕnd)*
to take care of; look after

treason *(trē′zə n)*
the betrayal of one's own country by
waging war against it or by aiding its
enemies

volunteer *(vŏl-ə n-tîr′)*
a person who performs or gives his
services of his own free will

Significant Statements from the Speeches of Patrick Henry

Caesar had his Brutus; Charles the First, his Cromwell; and George the Third may profit by their example. If this be treason, make the most of it.

Virginia House of Burgesses, 1765

The distinctions between Virginians, Pennsylvanians, New Yorkers, and New Englanders are no more. I am not a Virginian, but an American.

First Continental Congress, 1774

It is in vain, sir, to extenuate the matter. Gentlemen may cry peace, peace, but there is no peace. The war is actually begun. The next gale that sweeps from the north will bring to our ears the clash of resounding arms. Our brethren are already in the field. Why stand we here idle? What is it that gentlemen wish? What would they have? Is life so dear, or peace so sweet, as to be purchased at the price of chains and slavery? Forbid it, Almighty God! I know not what course others may take, but as for me, give me liberty or give me death!

Virginia Convention, 1775

A general positive provision should be inserted in the new system, securing to the states and the people every right which was not conceded to the general government. I trust that gentlemen, on this occasion, will see the great objects of religion, liberty of the press, trial by jury, interdiction of cruel punishments, and every other sacred right, secured before they agree to that paper.

Henry's Demand for a Bill of Rights,
Virginia Ratifying Convention, 1788